Standing Up to Peer Pressure

A Guide to Being True to You

Written by
Jim Auer

Illustrated by
R. W. Alley

ONE
CARING
PLACE

Abbey Press
St. Meinrad, IN 47577

For Rose, Jeff, and Jeannie.

Text © 2003 Jim Auer
Illustrations © 2003 St. Meinrad Archabbey
Published by One Caring Place
Abbey Press
St. Meinrad, Indiana 47577

Library of Congress Catalog Number
2003103128

ISBN 978-0-87029-375-7

Printed in the United States of America

A Message to Parents, Teachers, and Other Caring Adults

The phrase "peer pressure" frequently evokes images of teenagers dressing in outlandish fashions and experimenting with off-limits activities. But peer pressure is not exclusively the province of teens. Everyone feels it, from young children through adults, because it operates (one is tempted to say "preys") on the universal desire to be accepted and approved of. "Everybody else is doing it" begins at a very early age.

Although possibly blamed for too much, peer pressure deserves some of its villainous reputation—but also doesn't receive enough credit for its positive side. There are adults leading successful, productive lives who could justifiably say, "I wouldn't be here if it weren't for my friends." And there are adults languishing in prisons who could justifiably say the same thing. All of them started out as children who were well equipped or not so well equipped to distinguish between positive and negative influences and respond accordingly.

Preparing children to deal with negative peer pressure requires more than merely saying, "Well, just don't pay any attention to what other kids say." Two factors are crucial: instilling a conviction of what is right and wrong, and fostering a strong sense of self-worth and identity—this is who I am, and this is what I stand for. Every time a child sees an adult doing the right thing—and being happy for it—provides reinforcement for resisting negative peer pressure. And so is every affirmation of a child's worth and unique goodness.

It's not an easy task for adults to arm children with the necessary strength and judgment to respond appropriately to peer pressure. It requires patience, a willingness to repeat the message as often as needed in varying ways, and a readiness to deal constructively with the failures that a child will almost certainly experience. May this book help you guide the children in your care to prepare for any negative peer pressure that they will encounter.

—*Jim Auer*

What Is a Peer?

People are different ages. There are young people like yourself and older people like your parents and your grandparents. That's good. The world needs people of different ages.

People of about the same age are peers to each other. Someone who is about your age is your peer. People who are about your parents' age are their peers.

A peer might be a very close friend or just someone you recognize. Even people your age that you don't know at all are your peers.

Different Kinds of Pressure

Push on one arm with the other. That's pressure. You feel it with your skin and your body.

You can sense other kinds of pressure on the inside—with your feelings. When you want to win a game or a sport, that's pressure. When you want to do well in school, that's pressure, too.

We all need some pressure. It's good for us. It pushes us to get going. But pressure is not good if it pushes us in the wrong direction.

Feeling Good

It's normal to want to feel good. Many things help make that happen. One big way is when other people like you, and want to be with you, and think you're okay.

To help make that happen, it's natural to want to please your friends. You may want to be what they expect you to be. That's okay as long as they expect good things for you.

Peer Pressure!

When you feel that you have to be like your peers, and do what they're doing, that's called "peer pressure."

Sometimes peers actually tell you to be like them. They might say, "Let's all do this." Or they might say, "If you want to belong, you have to do that."

Sometimes you can just feel pressure inside yourself. If your friends dress a certain way or talk a certain way, you might feel that you should too—even if they haven't said that to you.

When Peer Pressure Is Bad

Sometimes your peers know that they are doing or planning wrong things. Some examples are smoking, stealing, using bad language, breaking things, or making fun of someone.

But if they can get others to do those things, then it lets them feel okay about it. They may try to get you to join them.

Much of the trouble kids get into comes from giving in to bad peer pressure.

Be Good to Yourself and Your Peers

God made you good, and God wants you to be nice to yourself and to your friends. That makes the world a good place.

If you follow your peers when they want you to do wrong things, you are not being good to yourself or to them.

When you do the right thing, you are being kind and loving to yourself and to others. Sometimes the kindest word you can say to your friends is "NO!"

What If It's Not Wrong?

What peers want you to do is not always wrong. Maybe they want to play softball, and you want to play soccer. Or they want to play a video game, and you want to watch television—or even do your homework!

Then you have to make a decision. Don't always insist on getting your way, but don't always give in either.

Friends should take turns.

Real Friends Respect Your Feelings

True friends like you just because you're you.

Peers who like you only if you do what they want are not true friends. They are not letting you be you.

The only thing you owe your friends is to be a good friend to them. You do not have to act like them in return for their friendship.

Prepare for Peer Pressure

There are many things that you need to be ready for. That way, when something happens, you can do what is right and be safe.

For example, it's important to know what to do if there is a fire, if someone gets hurt, or if you get lost in a store. That's called being prepared. Your parents can tell you these things.

You should prepare for peer pressure, too. Peer pressure is even more likely to happen than getting hurt or lost!

Start With Yourself

When friends like you, that's nice, and it feels good. But that's not what makes you a good and worthwhile person.

You are good and worthwhile all by yourself, just by being you. Feel proud of being you. Feel proud of knowing what is right and what is wrong.

If you feel that way about yourself, it will be much easier to say "No" when you need to.

Know What to Say

If peers pressure you to do something wrong or not good for you, say, "I won't do that" or "I'm not like that."

If they ask, "Why not?" just keep saying, "I won't do that." That's the ONLY reason you need! Just keep repeating it. Remember that you have a right to be you.

Sometimes they might make fun of you, or call you a name. That won't feel good. But knowing you did the right thing WILL feel good!

Find Support

Standing up to peer pressure can sometimes make you feel alone. But you really aren't. First of all, God is always with you. Ask God for courage to do the right thing.

Your parents may not be there when you have to say "No." But you can talk to them about it later, and that will help. You can talk to an older brother or sister, too, or maybe to a teacher.

Find peers who believe as you do about right and wrong. They can support you, too.

Be Like a Rock

Think of a rock and think of Silly Putty®.

A rock keeps its shape, even when something pushes against it. Silly Putty® just pushes in and takes the shape of anything it's put in. It's fun to play with, but that's not what you want to be like as a person.

When you stand up to bad peer pressure, you're acting like a rock. You're keeping your own shape, the way you were meant to be. You are being strong and firm. And that's a very good feeling!

Yes, You Can!

A big part of doing something hard is feeling and knowing that you can do it. Standing up to bad peer pressure is definitely not easy.

Tell yourself right now that you can do it. See yourself being strong with God's help. See yourself being the wonderful person God made you to be—even if your peers want you to be someone else.

Tell yourself, "When bad peer pressure comes my way, I'm going to be a rock!" Then feel proud of yourself for being yourself, and for standing up for what you know is right.

Jim Auer is a retired teacher and the author of fourteen books and several hundred articles and short stories. He and his wife live in Cincinnati, Ohio. They have two grown children.

R. W. Alley is the illustrator for the popular Abbey Press adult series of Elf-help books, as well as an illustrator and writer of children's books. He lives in Barrington, Rhode Island, with his wife, daughter, and son. See a wide variety of his works at: www.rwalley.com.